How to Get an Orgasm

Step by Step Instructions on How to Make Yourself Orgasm

(With or Without a Partner)

by Juliette Lane

Table of Contents

Introduction 1

Chapter 1: Differences Between the Climaxes of
Men and Women 7

Chapter 2: Learning to Love Your Body 13

Chapter 3: Getting Into the Right Mood 19

Chapter 4: How to Make Yourself Orgasm
WITHOUT a Partner 23

Chapter 5: How to Get an Orgasm WITH a Partner
.... 33

Conclusion 45

Introduction

Have you ever experienced a mind-blowing orgasm? That blinding moment of ecstasy during sex, when all your muscles tense up and incredible waves and waves of pleasure wrack your entire body? The sensations are so intense, you're prepared to die and ascend to the heavens at that very moment. Some women describe it as a powerful pleasurable sensation that takes them over the edge. The orgasmic experience varies from one person to another, but if you have never experienced these gratifying orgasms, you're missing out on life. Big time.

A number of women haven't truly experienced orgasm or the "Big O." Many of them will deny it though, because of embarrassment and the thought that maybe it's because their partners don't find them sexy enough. They'll fake orgasm with moans and cries of pleasure and their partners won't even know the difference. If you're one of these women, then you've got to know that you can do something about it. Having a sex life without experiencing orgasm is like living in a state of incompleteness, simply due to apathy and fear. Don't let this be the story of your sex life.

You have the right to enjoy sex with all those glorious orgasms and pleasures it provides. Don't think you're too old, either, to be dreaming of experiencing this slice of heaven on earth. No woman is too old to achieve orgasm. Reputable studies found out that the majority of women actually experience orgasm more during their midlife, and less – or not at all – during their earlier sex lives. With the use of lubes or lubricants, even post-menopausal women can obtain the type of orgasms described in the most detailed erotica books.

On the other hand, some young women have the incorrect impression that they should be able to climax easily during sex, only to find out later – to their dismay – that this is not particularly true. The proliferation of porn with steamy scenes of instantly groaning women in ecstasy has contributed to this wrong notion. It takes more than that for women to climax. And for any men out there reading this, take note, your partner may have been faking it. But good for you, since you're probably here to figure out how to give her a genuine orgasm, am I right? For women, now is your chance to learn how to make yourself orgasm, with or without a partner. This book provides detailed steps on exactly how to do just that. Let's get started, shall we?

Chapter 1: Differences Between the Climaxes of Men and Women

Before learning the steps of how to achieve orgasm, you need to be aware of the differences between a man and a woman's physiology and anatomy. This chapter will explain it simply, and in plain language for better comprehension. For men to know how to give their partner a genuine orgasm, they have to appreciate the anatomy of the female body. Likewise, for women, you really should understand how it all works too, in order to achieve orgasm.

Men Easily Achieve Climax

Because of their biological structure, men in general can easily climax through simple fondling, sexual stimulation, or sexual intercourse. The penis is composed of sensitive smooth muscles, blood vessels, and glands that are easily stimulated to make this possible. These body parts are all responsible for making the penis erect. Normally, men don't need a lot of stimulation to reach climax. Because of these easily interconnected anatomic structures, the male climax is often inevitable.

In addition, men can climax with women they don't feel any emotional attachment to because their ejaculation is unavoidable when they are aroused. Meanwhile, most women can only achieve orgasm with men they feel a certain attraction to. Also, for most women, the psychological aspect is crucial in achieving orgasm. The woman has to be in a positive mood to ensure that she comes during the sexual act.

Women Have Three Most Erotic Zones

Man's most erogenous zone is his penis. He can come just by fondling his penis. On the other hand, as a woman, you have an anatomy that makes it more challenging for you to climax. Your vagina has sensory receptors, but the clitoris and the G-spot are also erotic zones that have to be stimulated. Experts claim that you can climax by stimulating any of the three. However, some women need the stimulation of all for them to climax or achieve orgasm. You're responsible in choosing which erotic zone you want to focus on. Your clitoris is extra sensitive just like the penis of a man. It has more than 8,000 sensory receptors, far more than other parts of your vagina. So, where is this diamond of pleasure found? The clitoris is found at the uppermost portion of your vagina, right behind the folds of its outer lips.

Meanwhile, the Grafenberg Spot (G-Spot) is located at the upper portion inside your vaginal canal. You can find it by feeling for spongy tissue. Most parts of your vagina are smooth to your touch, but the G-spot has ridges of a sort. The G-spot corresponds to the male's prostate gland so its stimulation can produce climaxes like that of a man's prostate gland stimulation. During arousal, this G-spot swells and can produce sexual juices that enhance sexual pleasure due to friction.

The breast area of a woman is also an erotic zone that men should pay attention to. As a woman, you want to be thoroughly fondled, licked, and caressed on those body parts, don't you agree? During foreplay and orgasm, the breasts can hunger for those sweet caresses too, so don't ignore them guys!

However, men should understand that any and all of the aforementioned body parts are highly sensitive. Porn films showing the man exerting so much force in sucking and licking his partner's clit and breast are just not applicable, if he wants you to orgasm. These erotic zones should be handled with care. They should be attended to delicately, like fragile and easily broken items. Men should think of the clitoris as the female penis and be gentler when stroking and fondling it.

A woman's breasts are sensitive and should be fondled with gentle caresses and not massaged as if they are muscles. You can attest to the fact that when this happens, it gives you pain instead of pleasure. You must be bold enough to tell your partner when what he's doing is exciting versus hurting you. It's only through candidness that you can communicate correctly to your partner for a better sex experience.

Chapter 2: Learning to Love Your Body

Learn to love your body and yourself. A negative self-image is one impediment for you to get your much yearned for orgasm. How you perceive sex is also another factor that can prevent you from achieving your climax. Put aside all these biases and think of sex as a beautiful gift that you can share with your partner. It's something to be enjoyed and explored.

If your religious beliefs require you to refrain from promiscuity or pre-marital sex then, by all means, take heed of its teachings. It's your own conscience that counts. You can't enjoy sex if you'll feel guilty afterward, but don't ever perceive sex as something dirty and evil. Sexual intercourse is a unique union between two persons in body and soul. It's your perception and motivation that makes an act dirty or evil. You can start loving your body by using the methods below.

Believe That Your Body Is Beautiful

Face the mirror every morning, after taking a bath, and tell yourself that your body is beautiful. Closely examine your stark-naked body and orally say: "I'm beautiful. I have a beautiful body." Do this every day before getting dressed. Your body is beautiful because it's unique from anyone else's. No matter how much flab and unwanted bulges you have, you're still different from other people. You're you, and for that alone you're beautiful.

Explore Your Body

Know your erogenous zones by exploring your body. Close your eyes and run your fingers over your breasts and determine what type of touch excites you more. Do you want your breasts suckled or fondled directly, or do you want to first caress the tissue around them? What feels good? What doesn't?

Proceed to your vagina. Slowly caress the outer lip with your fingers and observe what portion of your vagina you feel the most sensation in. Open the folds of your vagina and feel for your clitoris. Play with it and determine what touch excites you the most. Insert your fingers inside your vagina and feel your way inside. What actions pleasure you the most? Remember them so you'll know beforehand. It will help you and your partner in climaxing during the sex act.

Masturbate Regularly

Men and women need a little wanking in their lives. Men most especially are advised to masturbate to release accumulated seminal fluids. With women, your body's exploration can precede your masturbation. Studies have shown that women who masturbated regularly orgasmed more easily than those who didn't. To help you achieve climax you need this essential activity. It will help you determine how to satisfy yourself and how your partner can satisfy you, as well.

You may want to experiment with vibrators and other sex toys. They come in various sizes, materials, designs, and styles. Some are designed more for vaginal stimulation and others for clitoral stimulation. You can also use your fingers to stimulate yourself to climax. Moreover, masturbation can allow you to master which buttons to push for you to come more pleasurably.

In addition, masturbation promotes health because it eases stress and tension. It releases endorphins that could prove harmful if not eliminated from your body. It can also serve as a good exercise for your body because you hyperventilate, your pulse quickens, and your blood circulation is enhanced.

Have a Healthy Lifestyle

You can't claim to love your body if you abuse it. You have to live healthily to take care of your body. Do this by eating a balanced diet composed of enough carbohydrates for energy, good fats such as fish and vegetable fat; proteins such as, soya, dairy products, lean meat; and essential vitamins and minerals. Your fruits and vegetable servings should be more than your meat servings. Sleep at least eight hours a day. Hydrate yourself properly, exercise regularly, and avoid drugs, cigarettes, and alcohol. These are all harmful to you.

Pamper yourself every now and then with a body massage, foot massage, or a day of relaxation. A relaxed and well-rested body will climax more quickly than a body that is stressed out. Staying healthy can increase the ease with which you attain orgasm.

Boost Your Mental Health by Being an Optimist

Your mind is extremely powerful. Being an optimist with a positive outlook in life will help a lot in your quest for the Big O. For most men, their mental state rarely interferes with their ability to climax because their bodies are wired that way. For you, you'll agree with me when I say that you'll have a hard time concentrating on sex, much less getting an orgasm, when you've got something bothering you. You have to be relaxed and comfortable to have sex and eventually come pleasurably.

When you think positively, you increase your chances of succeeding in all your endeavors. Positive vibes attract positive results. Visualize an image of you gasping in the throes of your climax and it will most likely happen.

Chapter 3: Getting Into the Right Mood

You have to be in the right mood before you can have a satisfying sexual intercourse. If you're expecting to have a sexual rendezvous with your partner, you'll have to prepare yourself, mentally and physically. You can prepare yourself by using these methods:

Read Erotica or Watch Sensuous Movies

Mentally prepare yourself early on by reading erotica or watching romantic movies. Soft porn can help if you find romantic movies boring. These can heighten your feeling of expectation. You can also imagine the thrilling things you'll do with your partner as the day drags on. Hence, when you meet with your partner, you're already wired up and aroused for more action. Most women are more difficult to arouse, so you should start your self-arousal hours before the actual sexual union.

Perform Kegel Exercises

Kegel exercises are pelvic floor exercises, which are believed to heighten orgasm in women. You can perform this by tightening the muscle that is responsible in stopping urine flow several times. You can do this exercise daily to strengthen your vaginal muscles. During intercourse, you can tighten the hold of your vaginal walls on his penis by doing the exercise. Most men enjoy the additional tightness.

Prepare a Private Cozy Place

The thrill of having sex in various positions, different venues, and at unusual times of the day makes it exciting. Nevertheless, if you finally plan to get that glorious orgasm you've been deprived of, you'll have to select a place where you can focus and feel comfortable in. How could you climax in the backseat of a car if you know that someone might happen upon you by chance? You'll have to experience unhurried sex to achieve your climax because if it's your first time, it can take a good amount of time to achieve that orgasm.

Observe Personal Hygiene

This is common sense. If you want you and your partner to enjoy all the pleasures that sex brings, you should clean your body thoroughly. Who would want to insert his tongue into a smelly vagina? Pay attention most especially to the areas which will be fondled, caressed, and kissed by your partner. Make sure you're ready for any eventuality. Have a lube handy, just in case.

Getting into the mood for steamy sex depends on your preferences. Make sure you have prepared yourself sufficiently to experience that mind-blowing orgasm.

Chapter 4: How to Make Yourself Orgasm WITHOUT a Partner

Now, how you can make yourself orgasm without a partner? You can only do this through masturbation. Lovemaking is an art and so is masturbation. If you have explored yourself before you've read this book, then you can do the following masturbation steps easily. First you should throw all your prejudices into the air so, you can enjoy loving yourself.

Step #1 - Get in the mood

First, mentally prepare yourself for your sexual exploration. You can play soft porn or soft music while masturbating to get you into the mood. Let go of stress and stay relaxed so your body will be receptive to sensual stimulation. The mind has a powerful grip on your body, so it must be prepared too. You can review the complete way to get into the right mood in Chapter 3.

Step #2 - Take a bath or a shower

Masturbating can introduce microbes into your body through your hands, so you have to be clean first. While bathing, you can begin fondling your breasts and vagina by taking your sweet time soaping them. Some women masturbate while taking a bath by using bidets trained on their clitoris, or soap to lather and explore their bodies. As a first timer though, this may be difficult for you and it might take a long time for you to come.

Step #3 – Find a comfortable place

After taking a bath, stay stark naked. If you have trouble being naked, you can cover yourself with a blanket, but this will restrict your movements. Find a cozy and comfortable place. The privacy of your bedroom is suitable for masturbation. A number of women get some kick from watching themselves in the mirror. You can do this to intensify your experience or you can simply close your eyes to savor your body's exploration. You can also watch a sexy video while masturbating or use sex toys such as clit stimulators, vibrators, and sex dolls. Use whatever you feel most comfortable with.

Step #4 – Explore the upper portion of your body

Begin touching yourself. Slowly let your fingers travel over your face. Relish the sensation of your fingers against your skin. Close your eyes and start by touching your eyes, nose, cheeks, and lips. Run your fingers lightly over them, imagining your lover doing it to you. Do this until you became familiar with the contours of your face. Imagine your partner kissing you on the lips. Run your tongue several times around your lips as if meeting the lips of your man.

You can also use a soft material of some sort such as a soft feather or a piece of silk to run over your skin. Rub the back of each of your ears with your index fingers. Do this slowly and teasingly.

Step #5 – Explore the lower portion of your body

Lower your exploration of your body to the area around your breasts. Lightly caress the area around the base of each breast with circling motions of your fingers or the soft material you have decided to use. Imagine your lover using his tongue to lick and his lips to rain kisses on that area. Do this several times until your nipples are eager for your touch. Then gently caress your nipples, tugging and circling them with your fingers. Imagine your lover's mouth is closing around them, sucking hungrily, circling them with his tongue, nibbling your nipples.

Step #6 – Explore your erotic zones simultaneously

While the fingers of one hand are caressing your breasts alternately, the fingers of your other hand can fondle your vagina. Don't go straight to your clit. Rub the outer lip of your vagina gently until you feel your arousal increase. Slowly part your vagina and stroke it with up and down movements, without touching the clit. This will heighten your climax. Insert one finger into your vaginal canal and slide your finger in and out.

Insert more fingers should you feel the need for fullness. If you have a vibrator, this is the time to insert it. Your clitoris is the small nub at the upper portion of your vagina just below your pubic bone. Refrain from touching the tip of your clit. Just use your fingers in making small circles around the tip. Do this until you feel that aching need for your clit to be touched.

Step #7 – Use your sex toy (if any)

Now, lightly run your index finger over the tip of your clitoris, while the fingers on your other hand or the vibrator are/is still going in and out of your vagina. Some vibrators have clit stimulators so you don't need to stimulate your clit with your fingers if you are using this type. Increase the speed and pressure of your finger on your clitoris according to the sensations you're experiencing. This will be up to you. It may be difficult to do this simultaneously, but with practice, you can learn the skill in fondling yourself. Using a pillow to elevate your buttocks can also help you achieve orgasm.

If you have done it properly, you should feel a sort of tension building up. Concentrate on what you're doing. Feel the glorious sensations produced by your own fingers. Focus on that tension until it becomes the central sensation and you feel all your muscles zeroing in on it like some unshakeable torpedo. You can also suck on something soft such as a soft rubber material or a teether to intensify your arousal.

Step #8 – Focus on the most predominant sensation

By now, all of your muscles should be straining to reach your orgasm. Continue fondling the erogenous zones that give you the most pleasure. Focus on these zones. Increase the tempo of your stimulation. You'll know you're on the brink of orgasm when your breath quickens and there's a sense of burning desire within you that wants to be satiated at all costs. That extreme desire can start from your clitoris and will spread slowly to all parts of your body. You're in the throes of your orgasm.

Step #9 - Surrender totally to your orgasm

When that intense pleasure finally comes, surrender totally to your orgasm. There's no specific rule on what to do in this instance, just follow what your body dictates and continue stroking or caressing the body part that needs it the most. Most often, the clitoris and the vagina desire more fondling, for you to achieve your full climax. Work with all items available for you.

Be prepared for an overwhelming sensation that can envelope your entire body. Some women experience momentary blindness when they come, some suck on their partner's neck, some scream uncontrollably like someone mad, some shudder with ecstasy. The experience differs for each woman, but all experience an encompassing pleasure that they have never experienced before.

Some women revealed that the G-spot orgasm is much more intense, and can even cause them to ejaculate. Look for that spongy ridge in the frontal wall of your vaginal canal and stimulate it by caressing and massaging it until you come.

Multiple orgasms can be achieved by women who have discovered early on how to make themselves come. You too can have multiple orgasms, if you get into the right mood, relax, and do the above steps properly. Of course, you can modify the steps and add activities that can increase your arousal. You may have sexual fantasies and sexual obsessions you want to experiment with. You're free to do so. Enjoy sex as you ought to.

If you still haven't gotten your Big O, then the problem may be psychological. You may have guilt problems about masturbation, or insecurity issues about your body. It's also possible you may have a medical issue. Perform all the steps three times, on different days, and in different settings. If it still doesn't work, then you should consult your doctor to find out about the possibility of an underlying medical condition.

Chapter 5: How to Get an Orgasm WITH a Partner

Once you've climaxed through masturbation, it should be easier to come with a partner. Be aware that before any of these things can happen, you must be in a relaxed and secure mood. You ought to be mentally synced and prepared to relish the delightful sensations that good sex provides. Below are steps that you can follow to achieve orgasm with your partner.

Step #1 – Prepare yourself mentally

These days the number of women climaxing is increasing. This is caused by the explosion of sexual awareness, sexual toys, and sex paraphernalia. In your case, you should prepare yourself mentally by preventing stress, anxiety, and any misunderstandings between you and your partner. Envision in your mind that you'll climax and that you'll enjoy superb sex with him.

You can start psyching yourself up hours before your sexual contact. Start thinking about the thrills and pleasures you'll savor later. This will start your love juices flowing. Envision yourself arching your back in the throes of pleasure from multiple orgasms. You can also read or watch sensual stories too.

Step #2 – Observe proper hygiene

Just like in masturbation, you have to be clean before making love. Pay special attention to your vagina, anus, and mouth. You'll never know where a steamy sex act can lead you. Set aside some lubricants too, in case your partner wants to use some tight openings. Of course, only do things that you're comfortable with. Communication between you and your partner is essential and you'll only enjoy sex if you welcome each act wholeheartedly.

Step #3 – Prepare a suitable venue

Sometimes, random sex is exciting. You can do it inside your van, in an enclosed area under the trees, at a secluded beach, or in your own garden. But, since you still haven't gotten your first orgasm, you should choose a place where you can totally relax and not be wary of intruders. It must be a place where you can stay in privacy for a long period of time. It can take a longer time for you to get your first orgasm. It's best to prepare for this eventuality.

The idea is to be free from any distraction, interruption or stress. Soft music, bubble baths, scented candles, and wine can all enhance the romantic atmosphere. Watching soft porn together while masturbating will stimulate both of you more. You can also massage each other sensually to enhance arousal.

Step #4 – Get into the mood

When your partner arrives, stay calm. Refrain from rushing into his arms and smothering him with kisses. Take it slow. The longer you prolong the foreplay, the more intense your sexual satisfaction will be. Eat. Supply sufficient calories to your bodies first. Drink some wine. Talk. Mental intercourse is just as powerful as sexual intercourse.

During these activities, make sure your bodies connect at certain points. When you talk to him, touch your fingers lightly over his thighs; whisper in his ears a few times, allow your nipples to brush his arm. Talk for a while until both of you feel relaxed and comfortable and the electricity of arousal is starting to build up. You can review Chapter 3 for more methods of getting into the mood.

Step #5 – You and he may need a shower

He may need to shower, and this is another chance for you to arouse him more. Don't let him climax in the shower though because then it will be over for you. You'll end up unfulfilled unless he decides to make you climax first. Help him soap up by stroking his body and slowly massaging him, focusing on his erotic zones: his nipples, balls, and penis. Allow him to give the service back, spread your thighs and let him lather between the folds of your labia while you soap his penis.

When he appears flushed and eager to begin, gently rinse his body and yours and lead him to your love nest. For men reading this book, take note that women can't climax as easily as you do. You'll have to arouse her more and this is done through breast, clitoral, and G-spot stimulation. Include the skin as a medium of sensual pleasure as it has receptors for feeling pleasure. The mouth and tongue are effective stimulators, use them. You or your partner can use a dildo or two fingers to stimulate your G-spot.

Step #6 – Prolong your foreplay

There are numerous ways to prolong foreplay and intensify your arousal. You could do this through fondling, caressing, and kissing. Kiss lightly while caressing each other's bodies. Intensify the kiss by nibbling his lower and upper lip, and then sucking his tongue. Your fingers should be busy stroking and fondling all body parts and going back to his major erogenous zones.

Let your tongue travel downwards, kissing every inch of skin it passes. Some men love their ears played with and licked. Rain kisses on his neck and chest, up to his nipples. Lead his hand to the part you want fondled too, so both of you will enjoy your foreplay. Suck his nipples lightly the way you want yours to be sucked. Then go down to his navel. Rain small kisses on his balls and suck them gently. Remember that these are extra sensitive to excess pressure. It's time to give adoration to his manhood.

Hold his penis upright in your hand and start licking and nibbling the crown, while your other hand plays with his balls. You can straddle him so you can receive your own share of loving. Slowly lower your vagina into his face and do the 69 position, one of the most popular sexual positions. This is advantageous for both of you because stimulation is done simultaneously, intensifying the arousal. Don't be shy to point out to your partner what turns you on the most.

Then run your tongue up and down his shaft, while alternately sucking and massaging it with your fingers. Handle his penis with care. Massage it gently and lovingly. Enclose the tip of his penis with your mouth and then go up and down his shaft with your mouth. Ensure that you're receiving the same arousal in your clit and vagina. Rub your clit into his face in a way that you find most pleasurable.

When you observe him moving in frenzy, slow your pace and lie down on your back. Gently push his face into your vagina. Let him continue sucking and licking your love hole until you feel that you're about to burst. If he's considerate, he'll willingly suck and render tongue service until you're ready for the penetration. Coax him to use his fingers in searching for your G-spot. He has to use his fingers to stimulate it.

Encourage him to concentrate on your clitoris and G-spot until you feel the tightening of your muscles and your intense desire ready to explode. You're now ready to climax. He can make you climax using his fingers and tongue, but if you want to simultaneously climax, you can proceed to the next step

Step #7 – Consummate the sexual act

Your body is in the throes of an orgasm, so you can now consummate the act. There are several positions for sexual intercourse. The most common is the missionary position, where he mounts you while you lay supine. You can spread your legs wide with your knees bent, while caressing his buttocks. There are a number of positions you can explore to get your orgasm. But you must take note that sufficient foreplay should be done first for you to achieve your goal.

- **Doggy** – Your man enters from the rear as you are down on all fours. This position as a great G-spot stimulator.

- **Butterfly** – You're flat on your back but your legs are hanging from the edge of the bed. You tilt your hips upwards and rest your legs on his shoulders as he stands at the edge of the bed opposite you. This is also an excellent position for G-spot stimulation.

- **Modified Missionary** – You're in the missionary position and then you place your legs at the center of his. He moves upwards a little bit to come in contact with your clitoris.

Your clitoris should be pressed against as he moves forward to thrust. You have to rotate your hips and grind against him, meeting his thrusts. Likewise, he must rotate his hips to rub the clit. This is a perfect clitoral stimulator, and will surely bring you to a wonderful orgasm.

- **Seated Scissors** – Your man is lying down and you're astride one leg facing the opposite direction. While you ride him you have to grind and slide against his legs and pubic bone to allow the clit, the G-spot, and the vaginal wall to rub against his body causing sweet friction.

- **Backseat Driver** – You're both seated. You're on top of him while facing the same direction. He holds your hips with both hands and lifts you up and down his penis. He can also lay down with you on top and your legs on each of his sides. You can face him too, so you can kiss and he can fondle your breasts.

- **Spoon** – You're both lying down and positioned like spoons. You're slightly higher so he can penetrate you from behind, while he caresses your nipples and breast and play with your clit. This is a wonderful position because all your erotic zones can be fondled.

There are numerous positions which you can discover if you're adventurous enough. Explore as many positions as you can before you give in to your orgasm. You can use ice to prevent your man from ejaculating early. Simply, touch the tip of his penis with ice for a few seconds. Many women have had multiple orgasms when they postponed their gratification.

You can modify the steps to come up with multiple ways to orgasm. Here are some of them:

- You can use a feather or something soft to stimulate yourself.

- Watch each other while you masturbate together before you proceed to sexual intercourse.

- Anal sex, while he stimulates your vagina with his fingers.

- Use dildos or sex toys to enhance arousal.

- Dance naked while exploring each other's bodies. Experiment with all sexual intercourse positions to find your favorite method.

Conclusion

Experiencing orgasm is a must for every woman. Not ever experiencing one is unthinkable. You must get an orgasm with a partner or without a partner. You're missing one of the joys of sex if you don't. So, apply all the tips that you've learned from this book and you'll surely get the exquisite pleasures that the Big O brings.

In addition, take note that the most important thing to remember is that you should be mentally prepared and attuned to attain sexual satisfaction. If your mind refuses to cooperate, you can't succeed in your endeavor of getting your much sought after orgasm. Have a positive mind-set and everything will turn out well.

Be mindful also not to contract any Sexually Transmitted Disease (STD) by observing safe sex and hygienic practices. Your health is still the foremost consideration. Be positive and confident. Smile, relax, and connect with yourself and your partner and experience the incredible ecstasy of orgasm.

Finally, I'd like to thank you for buying this book! If you enjoyed it or found it helpful, I'd greatly appreciate it if you'd take a moment to leave a review on Amazon. Thanks – and Happy Orgasming!

45236171R00029

Made in the USA
Middletown, DE
14 May 2019